The TRAGIC DEATH *of* ELEANOR MARX

Tara Bergin was born and grew up in Dublin. She moved to England in 2002 and currently lives in Yorkshire. In 2012 she completed her PhD research at Newcastle University on Ted Hughes's translations of János Pilinszky. She won the Seamus Heaney First Collection Prize 2014 for *This Is Yarrow*, published by Carcanet in 2013.

Also by TARA BERGIN from Carcanet Press

This is Yarrow · 2013

The Tragic Death *of* Eleanor Marx

TARA BERGIN

◇◇◇◇◇◇◇◇◇◇◇◇◇◇◇◇◇◇◇◇◇◇◇◇◇◇◇◇◇◇◇◇

CARCANET

First published in Great Britain in 2017 by
Carcanet Press Ltd
Alliance House, 30 Cross Street
Manchester M2 7AQ
www.carcanet.co.uk

A CIP catalogue record for this book is available
from the British Library: ISBN 9781784103804.

Book design: Luke Allan.

The publisher acknowledges financial assistance
from Arts Council England.

Supported using public funding by
ARTS COUNCIL
ENGLAND

for my parents and my brother

Contents

What is more precise than precision? Illusion.

Marianne Moore

The True Story of Eleanor Marx

I'm not going to tell you anything
That my psychoanalyst wouldn't tell you.
He too speaks in riddles.
He too proclaims we are all victims
Of our insurrections.
I will not stand up to him.

There are ten parts to the story...

The True Story of Eleanor Marx in Ten Parts

1.

Eleanor of the eight-hour day
Gets betrayed by Edward of the two faces.
She orders: chloroform, with just some traces
Of prussic acid – blue – a beautiful imitation.

2.

She says it's for the dog but she is the dog.

3.

The Housekeeper finds her dressed in white.
It's not her bridal dress, she's not a bride.
It's from her childhood. She lies as if asleep.
She has strangely purple cheeks.

4.

In her 'white muslin dress' she is laid out.

5.

The Coroner is exasperated with feeble Edward.
CORONER Was the deceased your wife?
EDWARD Legally?
CORONER Were you married to the deceased?
EDWARD Not legally.
CORONER What was her age?
EDWARD Forty.

(She was forty-three.)

6.

On Tuesday:
Fire –
But the Phoenix,
God of Suicide,
Doesn't rise.
And Edward doesn't claim her
Because now he has a real wife.

7.

So the urn that holds the ashes of the soft summer dress,
And of the woman who knew the power of the proletariat,
And of the chunk of poisoned apple that she bit under duress,
Are taken to the offices of the SDF.

8.

The offices are in Maiden Lane.

9.

And in the offices in Maiden Lane,
There is a cupboard with two glass panes.
And there they place her to remain
For years and years.
Her tears are dew
And she crushes nothing.

10.

Nearly all of this is true.

The Giving Away of Emma Bovary by Several Hands

If he asks me for her I'll give her to him.
If he asks for her, he shall have her.
If he asks for her, I'll give her to him.
If he asks me for her he can have her.
If he asks me for her, I'll give him her.
If he asks me I shall say yes.

Who Is He?

He used to scrape verdigris from copper coins and eat it.
Later when he wrote the suicide scene he vomited.
He lost his virginity to his mother's maid.
He was disgusted with himself, they say.
There is no mention of how the maid felt.
His sister was called Caroline, pronounced 'Caroleene'.
Caroline died when she was not yet twenty-three.
She lay in her wedding dress 'holding a white bouquet'.
He sat by her side all night, reading Montaigne.
At her funeral, the grave had been dug too thin.
The gravediggers stamped and forced the coffin in.
He wrote in a letter that the place where they stamped
was where her head must have been.
'The funeral was ghastly.'
There are links between his method and Stanislavsky's.
His first name for Emma was Marie.
He despised timidity.

Are You Looking?

She kept pricking her fingers and then sucking them.
She shivered as she ate; nibbling her full lips.
She had flushed cheeks!
Red-faced.
She walked in front.
'Are you looking for something?'
In church she was a show-off.
She showed them all her la-di-da;
her *fla-fla*.
On her shoulders: beads of sweat.
In her glass: the tip of her tongue.
She had perfect teeth.
She laughed at getting nothing.
Afterwards they went to her room.
In Spring: a wedding feast.
Their guest list numbered
forty-three.
Her dress was too long;
it picked up bits of grass
and thistles.

In Memory of My Lack of Feelings

I would rather die for love, but I haven't
FRANK O'HARA

What the Landlady says is that the pilot light has gone out.
Do you know what that means?
It means the whole building is freezing.
It means we keep our coats on and work in the cold,
hunching ourselves around our mugs of coffee for warmth.
It means we sit hunched like that, and gaze distractedly out
      at the trees,
thinking of nothing in particular apart from the cold.
I go on vaguely composing something weak,
some kind of comment on society –
but it is too weak –

And you know I could say:
'my chatter has a girl in it, she is opaque',
but that would be playing a game.
Or I could say: 'I walked up Dawson Street on a hot July day,
wearing a dress I thought you would appreciate',
but that would be playing a game.

Society has gone out, do you know what that means?

It means we all work here in the cold.
It means we sit here all hunched up,
looking at the fold in the white hills,
waiting for the workmen to come.
They will come, and I will fall in love with one of them,
and we will go to Dublin, and walk up Dawson Street,
me in a summer dress that everyone appreciates –

Oh you know I could have said, 'I never felt a thing',
your hands like soft clay; your hands like malleable clay,
soft and surprisingly afraid.
But I must say,
I cannot sympathise with myself: two-faced,
coiled around the serpent and saying, 'Does it feel OK?'
She is not what we thought; she was playing some kind of game.
And you came all that way.

The clock's reached 6 and we all know what that means:
it means the end of a working day.
Not for us.
I place my hand on the radiator – and nothing:
nothing has changed.

Answer to a Questionnaire

From the fat, tight fists of babies
I steal ideas; I steal similes;
and these I exchange for butter
and for bread.

For example, yesterday I said:
today we have the strange-sounding call
of a short-eared owl.
I said it to the baby.
This is the task for today, I said,
and I pleaded that the baby give me something.

The baby listened to the shriek of the owl.

Please, I said, or I will have nothing –
I will be bereft – this will affect you too.

The baby was a good little baby.
It opened its plump little fist,
and I stole from it:
goodies, high-pitched.
This morning I pawned it all
for some butter and some bread.

That's just one example.

To Dream of Horses

For a young girl to dream —

For a young woman to dream
that she sees a horse in human flesh,
descending on a hammock through the air,
and as it nears her house is metamorphosed into a man,
and he approaches her door and throws something at her
which seems to be rubber but turns into great bees

denotes:

miscarriage of hopes
and useless endeavours to regain what is lost;

denotes that she should be dealt with by wise authority;
foretells that she will be foremost in the favours of men.

If she was frightened, she is likely to stir up jealous sensations.

If after she alights the horse turns into a pig
she will carelessly pass by honourable offers of marriage,
preferring freedom until her chances are lost.

If afterwards she sees the pig
sliding gracefully along the telegraph wire,
she will – by intriguing – advance her position.

For a young girl to dream —

For a young woman to dream of horses

foretells:

she will have a mixed season of success and sorrow;
her interests will be injured;
she will be charged with making fraudulent deals with
unsuspecting parties;
undue passion will master her;
her desires will be loose,

and fortune will play her false.

The Hairdresser

My hairdresser is young
and she tells me things
no one else can:
about the different kinds of straightening tongs;
about the war in Afghanistan.

I sit with my hands in my lap,
in the ridiculous cape that she fastens for me
at the back. She stands at the nape of my neck

and I concentrate.

She tells me about her nan's hair –
which is coarse ('like yours') –
she tells me about colour, and tone;
she tells me about her boyfriend, the soldier,
who covered his ears at the party
and begged her to take him home.

I watch her in the mirror,
as she cheerfully takes hold of my hair,
and pulls it high up into the air;

I sit completely still in the swivel-chair,
and listen with great care
to all the things she has to tell me.

Expensive Sweetheart

Once I had a pocket full of change,
once I had a wallet full of notes,
once —
once I wore nothing round my neck,
I owned dresses and shoes and coats.
But now I've got a choker with an empty locket on it
and now I've got a cheque book with no cheques in it –
and now I'm so broke I live on promises:
they are the promises you tied around my neck;
oh now I'm so broke I open up the rubbish bags
and use what I threw out.
I bring it back into the house and use it –
that's how broke you made me.

The Workmen

Back and forth they go, from the van to the house,
leaning their ladders at angles, until bad luck
gathers beneath them like a vacuum.

She waits for the workmen to call her down.

They are awkward, she can tell.
She praises what they've done until their faces are hot,
and hers is too.

For something to do, she fusses over the baby,
who – like Gudrun in the snow –
is all yearning.

When the workmen leave to get their lunch
she sneaks outside and stands beneath their ladders,
holding little Gudrun, and thinking: let the bad luck come!

Whispering: behave yourself.
Don't you know it's good to have gentlemen
in the house?

Ode to the Microphone

Violence is such a lovely word.
I think you'll find I used it first –
I think you'll find I heard it first.
It wasn't what they wanted.
They wanted me – the fools – to wear a hat
but I fought them on that,
and won, of course.
Can you imagine?

Afterwards, I went home and did chores.
I wasn't a poet then.
Only a poet in rest.
So I say, don't I?
Again and again, if they should so wish.

It's the vowels I suppose.
(*into the microphone*)
O Vowels – how I miss you!

And I see I've made the news –
again and again, if they should so wish.

But it's still me on one side
and the fanatics on the other –
Lords of the Manor!
O how I envy them:
9 a.m. –
cigarette in one hand,
pen in the other,
surrounded by all their heroes and heroines.
On Fridays the bin men come
and pick up all their crumbs!

They hear the racket from their rooms.
I hear the roots of wild arum: growing down.
Lords-and-ladies of the manor!

And my oh my, they say now
that my speaking voice is sublime.
It improved when I crossed the Atlantic,
and spent a little time in the studio.

Afterwards,
I went home and did chores.
Because I wasn't really a poet then.
Only a poet in waiting.

Strange Courtship

These are the rules.

White lilac means: 'I am falling in love with you.'
Mauve lilac means: 'Are your feelings still the same?'

You give me the white today.
Then wait five days. Don't phone me.

On the sixth day I'll give you: mauve.
And then I'll see what's laid on my doorstep in the morning.

Mint, maybe.
Or laburnum.

It must mean something devastating –
or else I won't play.

Strange Commute

I tell the lights to hurry hurry:
little mo-mo's waiting –
I need to whisper *nighty-night!*
Not to mention you-know-who.
He needs to paint my small hand
white.

The Hospital Porter

The hospital porter is a philosopher
but he tells no one.

He goes home to his room every day
and tries to wash the smell of death off his blue clothes.

But he can still smell it –
even when his clothes are clean.

On his wedding day, his short hair was decorated with the
        blossom
that had blown down from the cherry tree.

But when he kissed his wife on their wedding night,
the petals were nowhere to be seen.

His new wife said: Don't worry! I didn't get married just for
        flowers.
But that wasn't true.

From then on, each time he worked the night shift
she placed another item in her suitcase.

By winter she was gone.

A Rented Room above the Registry Office

On Saturdays I share the threshold with brides,
with grooms,
who kiss and swoon beneath the flowers
and the flag
while I work in desperation
in the upstairs room.
From there I can hear the small crowd's cheer
and when I leave at night
I breathe the perfume of the guests,
and of the brand new wife.

On Sundays I step on bottle tops,
and see the pale confetti at the door.
Sometimes I find a tiny heart
stuck on my grubby sole.

Joseph's Palms

Last night Joseph held out his palms
and I saw how coarse they were.
Why are your palms so sore, Joseph?
I said, and I saw crossed lines.
I have been making these windows and doors,
he said, and this is what I get.
I said, but Joseph, if the strings on your hands
are rough and sore they won't play me so sweetly.
I liked your soft, high notes; your pudgy indoor coat.
And he said yes, I know.
And then Joseph did something very strange.
He placed his palms upon my hair,
and then upon my face,
and then he very gently held my throat.
There, he said.
Softness can be good,
but hardness is nearly always better.
I sobbed and said to Joseph,
what happened in the wood?
And for a moment
Joseph looked quite cruel.
I smelt the resin and the dust,
and felt a sudden, terrifying
lust.

Notes from the Arboretum

I would like to use the arboretum as a symbol, but of what?

If only I could sustain the energy of my imagination during religious and bank holidays.

I am afraid of happiness!

How can a bird native to China survive here?

I would like to be able to say that I am unhappy because of circumstances beyond my control, but this is not the case.

I look into the eyes of the Saker Falcon and ask: What did you see in Iraq?

The Saker Falcon gives me nothing. Everyone wants a bit of him.

I go back to the awful arboretum several times.

This is despite the fact that the entrance fee is so grossly excessive it prevents me from enjoying the experience in any way.

Each time I return, I go straight to my scornful friend, the Falcon.

I look into its eyes and say:

At night we wander freely – half free – at the sides of our grandparents and among the grounds of famous American Universities.

I whisper through the wires:

It's hard to know if the dreams are symbols of what has passed, or what is yet to come.

He sits in his tight leather hood.

Come on, Falcon – all I've got are these notes for a poem.

Not an actual poem.

The Stenographer

'After the quotations will come the accusations [...]
It exists only in cut-outs and commentaries [...]
We see her downfall in the forest [...]
She dies in all the glamour of her youth [...]
I am passing over nothing.'

Faithful Henry

Faithful Henry looked in the mirror and said to himself:
Do you have any faith in yourself, Henry?
He felt an iron band breaking from around his heart.
What's that cracking sound, Henry?
called his wife from their bed.
It's just an iron band breaking from around my heart,
he called back.
Oh, she said.

Faithful Henry turned back to the mirror and said again to himself:
Do you? Do you have any faith in yourself, Henry?
He felt another iron band breaking from around his heart.
What's that cracking sound, Henry?
called his wife from their bed.
It's just another iron band breaking from around my heart,
he called back.
Oh, she said.

Faithful Henry looked in the mirror a third time.
Do you have any faith in yourself, Henry? he asked himself again.
He felt a third iron band breaking from around his heart.
But why are all those iron bands breaking, Henry?
his wife called from their bed.
Because I feel so happy, he replied.
Oh, she said.

Faithful Henry stared at himself in the glass.
No, he said very quietly, you don't.

Susie's Secret

Susie has a little heart;
It needs a little key.
To those who cannot find it
Susie says:
Don't bother me.

I have it;
Do you want it?
Susie will not guess.
Just close your eyes,
And think that I am Susie
Saying:
Yes.

Tamer and Lion

Thomas, I won't give up on you,
even though they are all saying that you are cruel and corrupt.
Anyway, there is a relationship between exerting cruelty
and oneself being trapped:
I know this because I sometimes feel that you are the rat
and I am the dog; but also that I am the rabbit
and you are the fox. They turn them inside out,
did you know that?
But you too suffer, Thomas.
I know because I've seen your brow,
which is impenetrable like the Lion's brow;
I know because I've seen your mouth,
which is half-open like the Lion's mouth;
wet;
somehow sensual;
I know because I've looked into your eyes,
which are like the Lion's eyes in colour,
and perhaps also in their heartlessness.
Thomas, even the tilt of your head recalls the tilt of the Lion's
        massive head!
But while – like the Lion – you are to be feared,
you are also fearful.
Aren't you?
You have the ability to do great hurt, Thomas,
but you also carry within you a great hurt.
Don't you?
I hope you do, Thomas.
I do.

Renting Emily Dickinson's Bedroom by the Hour

I don't want to do anything.
I just want to watch.
I want to see what she saw.
I don't want to touch
or be touched;
I want a different kind of pain.
If I can get it once
I won't come back again.

Lorraine

I didn't tell you there were monkeys.
They stroked Lorraine's red hair
and –
she said –
her breast.
The rest of us just turned away disgusted
then Lorraine cried out:
It bit my hair!
But hair doesn't bleed,
does it,
so none of us believed Lorraine.

She became a sculptor:
strange, incomplete women;
toy boats.

When we met again
aged forty or forty-three
she said to me:
do you ever wonder
if all our memories of childhood
are just our childhood dreams?

Dying

I waited until everyone was out of the house.

I waited until there was nothing on the horizon;
nothing in the diary;
nothing in my notebook;
nothing at my writing hand at all.
Until my writing hand was hardly ever being used.

Then I got everything ready:
the stopwatch;
the deep, stainless steel bowl;
the bottle of salt;
the packet of blue powder.

Back went the dial on the old stopwatch,
until it was tight and began to count me down.
In went the warm water.
In went the five tablespoons of salt.
In went the packet of grainy blue dye.
Then in went my stiff wooden hand –
in went my out-of-fashion hand!

And it held itself down.
For twenty-two seconds, and then another twenty-two,
it agitated itself and drowned itself out in the blue.
It lost oxygen and turned the colour of the sea –
the sea from a foreign point of view –
it turned a dark, cold, airless blue,
as if it had not breathed for some time –

and just as it assumed the appropriate shade;
just as it turned into a deep and dying blue,

the stopwatch gave way and rang its alarm.
I lifted my hand up from the sink:
it looked shrunken. It looked taboo.

And for all that week I admired my new hand.
I sat at the table, leafing through free magazines,
proud of finally taking the time to renew it so thoroughly.
I spoke on the telephone, distracted by the newness of my hand.
I sat at the computer, trying it out,
awkwardly tapping all of the wrong keys.

Yes, I thought, this is very me.

'If I Love One I Can't Love Two'

When I'm with X I have no thought of Y.
But when I'm with Y I start to suspect X of trickery.

This encourages me to give myself to Y completely.

But then Y takes and takes,
until I start to think that X is actually nicer than Y;
that X is the one who truly loves me.

X has no money whereas Y is rich.
It shouldn't matter, I know!

But still.

Eeny, meeny, miny, mo –

Painter My Valentine

On Valentine's Day
my Valentine –
mine –
has cut his throat;
his Adam's apple's
bled a little
on his t-shirt,
which is white,
like all the fields
today, Monday.

Yesterday, Sunday,
he nailed a canvas –
white –
onto the wall
in preparation for the night.

Tomorrow, Tuesday,
out will come
sap
from his unhealed throat.

What will happen to my love
on Wednesday?

Bachmann's Warbler

Who counts the money?
Who sits behind a shield
and tells me the phone isn't safe?
Who has her lunch at one?
Who shows me what I've done
and makes me poorer, richer,
whatever I want?
Who demands my number and my key?
Who is always *warning* me?

Students –
Who is the nice lady in the bank?
Is she Death? Is she Love?
What *feeling* is she? What *state* might she be?
Let's think of a different word for melancholy.

Can we? Shall we?

Oh Students –
I must address you from my deathbed,
from my deathchair, from my deathdesk.
I must stand at the window,
and address you thus:
don't refuse to taste the sweet –
to taste the salt –
Don't refuse it always.

If I was the cause of your unhappiness
I cannot apologise.
I was – of course – the cause of mine.
I said yes. I said yes several times.

Remember this: yes is not always the right answer.
But it might be. How will we know?

Oh –
I have struck,
twenty-one times,
the lighthouse in the Florida Keys;
I have been shot by the plume hunter;
I have not made a nest for ninety-five years;
I am on the verge of extinction;
I have begun my decline –

And can you hear me,
Students of the Heart's Revolution?
I speak to you in a voice
no one has heard for decades.
I speak to you through lips
of salt and sugar.

Now, answer me:
Who changes the currency?
Who stamps the receipts?
Who says the gesture of authenticity
is also an aesthetic gesture?
Who?

Sweet Isis

Down by the banks of the sweet Isis,
Underneath the weeping tree,
My lover gave me an emerald bracelet
To prove he'd not forgotten me:
Six green hearts for jealousy!
I put it on; bright green on white.
'Not nice,' I whispered, secretly,
But held my wrist out prettily,
And kissed him on the lips –
I too, I knew, could play these tricks.

We wandered off, and sweet and free
To others we appeared to be.
But in the water deep and green
We looked,
And saw our hearts most mean,
And hard, and weeping
Like the willow.

Making Robert Learn Like Susan

Everybody wants Robert to learn like Susan,
but there are always more Roberts than Susans,
aren't there?
Blaming Robert isn't helpful.
Susan is by nature a deep learner:
it's easy for her.
She's not like Robert,
trying to show off with big words like
opaque
or transubstantiation.
Silly Robert.
He has memorized them from a book!
He doesn't know their real meanings!
Because Robert is a *surface* learner,
whereas Susan is *deep*.
Blaming Robert isn't helpful.
What we need
is to take all the Roberts from this world
and make them Susans.

Portrait of a Writer

Hold it, says Gisèle.

She presses, then releases,
and Virginia knows that her soul has been taken.
She knows that everyone will see it.

Gisèle is very used to this reaction.

She presses
it's a violation
then releases.

Drama Lessons for Young Girls

Remember:
in a stage play every scene is driven by OBJECTIVES.
Every scene is driven by WHAT A CHARACTER WANTS.
DRAMA is created when objectives clash.

Here we see a young girl
cast as a young girl from the Acropolis,
moving elegantly forward,
and carrying an offering in her outstretched hand.
She is a figure in the act of worshipping.
She is holding out her hand –

but the outstretched hand is missing,
and where it was is a stump of alabaster.
And her nose and her chin are missing,
and where they were are two stumps of alabaster.
The lips are red, and the eyes are wide,
so she still looks like a pretty girl.

And her goddess is missing.
Athena has run off with the wolves.
They barked and howled and off she went.
Where has she gone?
What is it all meant to signify?

Remember:
in a stage play BAD DIALOGUE is expositional.
Characters OFTEN LIE.
They lie as a way of HIDING TRUTHS.

And hundreds of girls came bleeding to the door!
Their right hands outstretched!

But the grown-ups pulled the grille, and said:
you're naughty.
So the young girls,
cast as naughty young girls from the Acropolis,
left –
just with some things missing.
Their lips were red and their eyes were wide,
so they still looked like pretty girls.

Remember this.

When the stakes grow in intensity,
it is known as BUILD.
DELAY is a dramatic device.
SUBTEXT is a character's DEEPEST SECRETS.

Tamer and Hawk

He has a table for the bird.
He strokes the bird.
He feeds it morsels, snuggles with it.
They have their sweet nothings.

The bird is wired with little bells.
It won't take fright:
it doesn't want to hear the jingle-jangle,
does it?

No.
The tamer keeps the hood on.
That's right.

Talking to Anne-Marie after the American Election

Wednesday morning, bright at the office after the catastrophe,
I said: What do you make of the catastrophe, Anne-Marie?
And I sipped my coffee, and opened up my emails, and so on
        and so forth,
until eventually Anne-Marie said from her desk:
Do you want to know something?
My name's not actually Anne-Marie.
And I said: What?
And she said: My name's not actually Anne-Marie. It's Anne.
And I said: But we've all been calling you Anne-Marie for years.
Everyone calls you Anne-Marie.
I know, she said. But it's actually Anne.
Just Anne? I said. No 'Marie' at all?
And she said: No. No 'Marie'. Just Anne.
Jesus, Anne-Marie, I said, I can't see you as an Anne at all.
You're definitely an Anne-Marie.
To ye I am, she said,
but to me and mine I've always been an Anne.

A pause.

And then I said:
So what now? What now as Anne?
Now, she said, after yesterday's catastrophe,
nothing is safe,
and I can hold off my breakdown no longer.
Because as Anne, she said, I am unbalanced;
impetuous; eaten up with jealousy;
I sit for hours with Judith under the laurel tree,
eyeing up other women's babies –
love, for me, you see – for *Anne* – is unforthcoming.
Ah now, I said, but she was having none of it.

No, she said, I'm too verbose. Too all-show.
But where will you go, Anne-Marie? I said,
and she said: It's Anne. And I don't know, yet.
Perhaps Huston, Texas.
There's a psychiatrist there who understands.
And I said: Good on you!
And sure if you've room in your suitcase,
won't you take me too?
Or maybe I'll go somewhere else, said Anne-Marie.

And with that she stared down at her computer screen,
and I stared down at mine.
And that was the end of our conversation,
on the morning of Wednesday, November 9.

Diary Entry, Easter Monday, Suicide Day

I know what today is:
Monday, a Public Holiday.
I know that no one will come.
Bye-bye public holidays when no one comes.
Full house on Tuesday!

Appointment with Jane Austen

Blushing in a manner out of keeping with my age
(my greying hair, my falling face)
I entered Greyfriar's Inn.
I was blushing, and out of keeping with my age.
In I went, making my foolish entrance,
folding down my umbrella self-consciously –
aware of the locals at the bar with their gin
and their small talk –
and walked right up to the barmaid,
somewhat brazenly, I thought. One glass of beer,
I said to her, and she, smiling kindly,
pulled it. I stood and waited.
I waited for them all to stop their fond,
drunken reminiscences,
for them to stop putting forth their opinions,
and to turn to me and say – in an accusatory way –
What are you doing here? On a Wednesday night?
Unaccompanied?
With an accent we can't quite identify?

I waited ready:

Why am I here? I would say.
I am here as an imposter, an outsider,
a reluctant admirer of your lovely daughter Jane –
I am here for my Lecture on the Picturesque,
to learn of sidescreens and perspectives,
to learn of window tax and syntax – and 'ha-has' –
for harmless gambling in the parlour,
wearing mittens and handworked collars and a pretty
          amber cross –

I am here to steal a pistol and a spoon found underground,
to rob the peacock feathers streaming from the silly boy's
    crown –
I am here, I would say, for *sensation* –
For sensation? they would say, and I would say:
Yes! *Painful sensation of restraint or alarm*!
Oh ye patrons of Greyfriar's Inn, I would exclaim,
I am here to meet your high-waisted Jane,
to embrace her as my comrade; as my brother-in-arms!

I stood and waited. But the good patrons of Greyfriar's Inn,
they never said a thing; just continued talking amongst
    themselves,
quietly reminiscing. I paid the barmaid and turned my head.
I looked out at the wet; I looked out at the southwest rain,
and the redbrick houses. I watched the famous silhouette
gently swinging back and forth above the gate.
I raised the glass to her impassive, sideways face.
Nothing ventured. Nothing gained.

The Hunchback in Golden Swan Park

I'm not crying for him;
that's what I say,
but Pity & Desire are close to one another.
Isn't that a dangerous similarity?
The kids bring him things: little prizes little treats.
They are not too cruel, not like in the old days.

Hey Mister, let me caress your face;
let me lie with you in your sleeping bag over by the gates.
The golden swan isn't true, not like you, she is a fake.
Out of place, where warm air from the subway
comes up in waves.
It smells of chlorine and no one beautiful stands there.

And there are nurses but they don't wear white.
They dress like janitors; they are not so feminine.
They tell me CPR has changed:
mouth-to-mouth's no longer necessary.
It's the beating hands that count.
1, 2, 3, 4, 5, 6, 7

It's 8 a.m.
Far away in England,
the seagulls are screaming,
even though it's as dark as night.
They scream down alleyways like girls in flight.
Old men wake and wonder.
They are only five hours away from light.

Mask

It won't help if I tell you this but it might.
I was making this mask for the children.
I was holding the white face in my hand,
its underside around my palm.
I was painting it.
It was not at all frightening.
But as I was doing it I was thinking,
This is interesting.
This is like a physical manifestation of what I do.
I mean: *what I do daily in my room.*
I held the face in my hand and painted it.
Then I tried it on and said What do you think?
Everyone squealed and screamed.
They all wanted to make one.
Some of the paint got on my hair.
No one cared.
Soon all the kids had made a mask.
They put them on and went around screaming.
Some of them got paint on their hair.
No one cared.
They were both themselves and strangers.
That's all they wanted.

Poem in Which I Am Samson and Also Delilah

I am Samson, but I am also Delilah.
I say to myself: Cut off all your hair!
Then I say: No.

I am in a bad way.

Two weeks ago, as Samson, I went crazy.
I got myself drunk and killed a small deer.
I buried it in the hedge.
When I went back, sober, to apologise,
I noticed that bees had made honey in its carcass.
I ate some of the honey – which I do not like –
and gave some to my parents.
That night,
my wife turned to me with a sick expression on her face.
What is it, I said?
She said, What is sweeter than honey?

She knew what I had done.

I ran away, and became desperate.
As Delilah,
I flirted with the bank manager.
He lent me £1,100.
I used it to try and bribe the barber: Come on, come on!
But then I phoned up with excuses and lies:
tied myself up with string, with rope,
and remained undecided – worse, unbroken.

Tired out, I fell asleep to my own singing.
In my dream, I cut off all my hair.
At last! I said in my dream.

At last I did what I wanted!
But it wasn't real.
In the morning, I looked in the mirror.
I saw Samson, relieved.
I saw Delilah, disappointed.

And so it goes on.

My right hand grasps the scissors.
My left hand twists them loose.

Nine Footnotes

[1] literally: 'I was full of trepidation'.

[2] The music in the background is Chopin's *Ballade* No 1. Op. 23.

[3] This list of words conveys a certain sense of hope.

[4] i.e. he is not actually a stranger.

[5] i.e. 'I am not comfortable in a suit and tie'.

[6] OED definition of 'showmanship' or 'the art of the showman'.

[7] i.e. a storm is taking place *inside* the hurricane lamp.

[8] Meaning 'I haven't even given a thought to his [the child's] fever'.

[9] Here, the phrase 'a dry spell' does not refer to the weather.

On Not Picking Mushrooms with a Famous Writer

Unreasonably nervous of poisons,
I stayed home.

That night he fried them in hot butter
and ate them from the pan.

'You don't know what you're missing,'
he said.

'Oh but I do,' I said, watching with envy.

Insomnia

It means habitual sleeplessness
but I'm going to use it anyway.
I'm going to use it while I have my say:

I bit their hands,
I looked into their mouths –
do you know what I'm saying?
I made a mistake –
I took Christ's Tears
and placed them with the peelings
and the bones.
Yes. That's how it was:
in the one hand I had a flower,
and in the other hand I had a flower,
and I didn't know what to do.

And then the radio's biblical news about a mountain,
and the breaking voice of a man:
We will fight on the Mountain.
The tears of the Messiah will not have been shed in vain.

It's not too late!

And out behind the gate I sank my hands
amongst the peelings and the bones,
and found at last Christ's bruised and stinking tears.
I laid them out to dry upon the stones.

And the radio still speaking,
explaining to me that the meaning of hope
is bound up with waiting.
What a sentence!

Do they know what they are saying?
Do they know how they are keeping us awake?

Of course they know.
They have experience of life.
We do too, but not so much.

The Method

Everything I do, I do in order to get something.
For example: Jane.
I want Jane, but she doesn't want me.
Now, everything I do,
I do in order to get past the obstacles to Jane.

Why doesn't Jane want me? Perhaps she fears me.
Why does Jane fear me? Perhaps I am violent.

What is violence? What is power?

I hide my needs.
I act like a different person.
I do it in order to get what I want.

Which, in this case, is Jane.

Rehearsing Strindberg

Miss Julie enters in travelling clothes.
She enters in these clothes so that we know
that she is going, and will soon be gone.

Miss Julie enters in travelling clothes
and she enters in these clothes so that we know
that she is going, and will soon be gone.

She is nervous throughout the dialogue.

Miss Julie enters in travelling clothes.
She enters in these clothes so that we know
that she is going, and will soon be gone.
She is as white as a corpse, and –
'forgive me, but your face is dirty.'

She has a birdcage which is covered by a cloth.

Again:

Miss Julie enters in travelling clothes.
She enters in these clothes so that we know
that she is going, and will soon be gone.
She is as white as a corpse, and –
'forgive me, but your face is dirty.'
She has a birdcage which is covered by a cloth.
Inside the birdcage is Serina –
the little greenfinch: her only friend.
The only one who loves Miss Julie.

Again:

Miss Julie enters in travelling clothes.
She enters in these clothes so that we know
that she is going, and will soon be gone,
and she is as white as a corpse, and her face –
she washes her face in the rising sun –
It's Midsummer.
She has memories of lilacs and birch leaves.

What's under the cloth? What's in the cage?

It's Serina the little greenfinch: her friend.
The only one who loves Miss Julie.
But: 'I won't leave her for strangers.'
And: 'I'd rather she was dead.'

Again:

Miss Julie enters in travelling clothes.
She enters in these clothes so that we know
that she is going, and will soon be gone.
She is as white as a corpse, and –
'forgive me, but your face is dirty' –
but she washes her face in the morning sun –
and she is nervous –
she is nervous throughout the dialogue.

And when she takes the little bird out of its cage
she kisses it: 'Oh poor little Serina!
'Are you going to – leave your mistress?'
And she takes the little bird out of its cage and
she kisses it: 'Oh poor little Serina!
Are you going to die now, and leave your mistress?'

And Miss Julie enters – *in an ecstasy* –
inside the birdcage – beneath a cloth –

and 'You spit at me, and won't let me wipe it off – '
and the lackey puts the razor in her hand.
'It's horrible.'
And the lackey takes the bird to the chopping block.

Again:

Miss Julie enters –
to the chopping block –
'you are too handsome' –
beneath the cloth –
'I almost fear it' –
he lifts the axe –
'It's horrible' –
but 'kiss my hand and thank me!' –
and 'kiss my hand and thank me!' –
and it's too late – or it's too early –
and then the lackey puts the razor in her hand –
and –
'am *I* to obey *you?*' –
and
'are you going to –?'
and –

Miss Julie enters in her travelling clothes.
She enters in these clothes because she knows
that she is going –
and will soon be gone.

Again:

The Sad Tale of Hansel and Gretel

You know how Hans lost his bride,
Don't you?
He took everything literally.
He went too close.
He listened to the instructions –
But not in context.

Hans couldn't think how awful Gretel would feel
By the maimed faces of the sheep and cows;
By the touch of the bloody eyes
On her soft white cheeks.

Poor Gretel.
Poor Hans.

When he threw the eyes and they landed on her
She shivered and ran away.
Hans should never have put eyes on her like that.
She was his sister.

He knew something was wrong.
He knew three times.

Poor Hans.
Poor Gretel.

Both yearned for oceanic feelings of dissolution.
Both searched for their crumbs on the path.

They'd gone too far.
The magpies had already gobbled them up.

Wedding Cake Decorations

A small white wife
with a small white face;
a thin white groom
on a round, white base.

They have no shoes
because they have no feet:
their maker thought them obsolete.

They cannot run away!

The married man
and his married wife
are stuck this way.

Let's hold each other tight,
they say.

So they hold each other
all through the day,
and all through the
frightening night.

Secret Resignation

First I'll take: the view of the hospital.
The week after that: the loud helicopter on its pad.
On my last day, I'll steal that tiny pair of shoes,
the ones that sit in the glass cabinet.
Oh, I'll make use of them,
don't you worry!

If / *Then*

If you are walking on blood,
then I am Sonia;

and if you are suffering from hypertension,
then I am Joanne;

and if you are surrounded by singing birds,
then I am Miriam;

and if you are a deserted village,
then I am Natasha;

and if you are blue for Buddhists,
then I am Vera;

and if you are the lucky John Smith,
then I am Helen;

and if you are a satyr,
then I am Joan;

and if you are saying you're in love with me,
then I am definitely saying that I'm in love with you.

Notes from the Sanatorium

It would have been better to cross with the nuns –
like A—— did in Rome –
like P—— did that time he was far from home –
to wait, and cross with them anonymously!
I have always had far too much of myself in me.
In my heart. In my chest.
And even though it's not actually late –
not in the real world –
it feels late.
But who wants to listen?
Not me.

You see it's not a safe road
but at the same time it's not daring.
At times I fear the link is broken, or breaking.
At times I fear all my letters are lost.

Frugal living has a high cost.

I don't talk to my lover, or to my friend who has emigrated.
I don't talk to my brother, or to my friends – not since I
       emigrated.
I only talk to faces I don't know,
and their thoughts don't always show.

I longed to be a —— of great renown,
but I can see that I needed to sell it better.
It's all I can do, and yet, lately, I feel I can't –
the sick eye, the sick ear.
My limitations are: I have no foresight.
I cannot hear.
Not the subtle noises.
And this is how it feels.

If everything we wanted was the same,
if everything we wanted was right,
how could anyone be renegades?
How could we really know the night?

After times like these,
I want to fall on my knees.
After talking like this,
I blush to the roots of my hair.
To the roots of my soul,
the soul I pass around everywhere.

'Oh My Little Eleanor...'

Oh my little Eleanor
Your favourite flower is all flowers
And your favourite colour is white
But oh my little Eva
Your favourite flower is orchid
And your favourite colour is night –

Karl Marx's Daughters Play on the Ouija Board

LAURA   Here take this pencil,
and poke it through the heart;
that's right,
through the little hole in the centre,
yes, and place your hands on the little heart,
and now let it move your hands around,
you must let it move your hands around;
don't try to control it,
or it won't work.
Don't try to make it up;
let the heart spell out the answer.
Ask it something, Eleanor.

ELEANOR Does my lover spend the rent on cigarettes?

LAURA   It's spelling Yes, Eleanor.

ELEANOR Does he tell fibs when I undress?

LAURA   It's spelling Yes again, Eleanor.

ELEANOR Is he the cause of my unrest?

LAURA   It's spelling Yes, Eleanor.

ELEANOR Has he married his mistress?

LAURA   Eleanor! It's spelling YES!

The Tragic Death of Eleanor Marx

Mademoiselle:
little
Frau-lein:
little
daughter
you have left your mark:
a little jottings; a little paper;
a little ink on the sides
of the mouth.
What did you think?
That it was nice?
That it was easy?
La clef turned in the lock:
that bit is easy, but the rest?
What happened next?
Ah yes, this is what turned your head:
She –
Mrs Bored, Mrs Why-Did-I-Marry –
she went over / went directly / she went straight over
to the third shelf,
so well did her memory serve her
and she took down / and she seized / and she *sasit*
     the blue jar
– and then and there – she –
and this is where you think *Me* –
or rather, *I* –
seized the jar – *I*
tugged at the cork /
tore out the stopper /
pulled out the cork /
pulled out the stopper –
and stuck her plunged in

my hand –
and then withdrawing, and then with taking, and then with
        scooping
she drew it out / she scooped it up / I took it out
in her glove /
in my fist /
in a hand full of powder,
and there and then / and then and there /
began to eat.
I want it she said, didn't she?
Give it to me.

Bride and Moth

Every sadist needs a masochist.

What queer songs Green Peter sings –
but of course he is both attractor and deceiver:
I mean, he thinks they are the same thing.

Now at the start I thought I was Hawk,
or Coxcomb, or Cream-bordered Chinese;
I thought I was Crimson,
but you thought of me differently:
a Common Footman; a Common Lackey;
a Common Yellow Underwing.

But I could never have been these things.
What cruel songs Green Peter sings.

Because I thought I was Emperor,
while you thought I was Eyed,
and I thought I was Fox,
while you thought I was Feather-flied,
and I swore I was Garden, and Ghost-swift, and Gypsy-pied,
but you said I lied:
I was Hook-tip, you shouted, and Iron.

I cried, and said no I was Kentish Glory,
and Jersey,
and Lutestring:
I showed you the tops of my new white stockings.
But you turned aside,
and spat that I was a Lappet; a Lesser;
I fell to my knees at the Registrar

and said that Oleander was my name.
You laughed and said it was Old Lady.
I clutched at your tails:
I am Pale; I am Peach-blossom, I wailed,
No, you said, you are Pebble, and Puss.
I picked myself up.
I said I was Reed and Rosy, and Satin and Scarce.
I held grandly my white satin purse –

But every masochist needs a sadist!
sang hand-tied little Peter,
as rehearsed.

Notes

The True Story of Eleanor Marx in Ten Parts · Eleanor Marx, daughter of Karl Marx, was a pioneering socialist who fought tirelessly to secure workers' rights. She was also the first official English translator of Flaubert's *Madame Bovary*. In March 1898, Eleanor Marx committed suicide in a manner similar to that of the novel's title character. She had just learned that her partner Edward Aveling, with whom she had lived for almost fourteen years, had secretly married another woman called Eva Frye. Shortly after discovering this fact, Eleanor gave her housekeeper a letter requesting poison from the chemist; the same type used by Emma Bovary to kill herself. In this letter, to avoid suspicion, Eleanor wrote that the substance was for the dog. Before she died, she changed into her favourite summer dress. The inquest into Eleanor Marx's death took place on Saturday 2 April; Edward Aveling was the first witness; the inquest report was published in several newspapers at the time. See Rachel Holmes, *Eleanor Marx: A Life* (2014).

This is an engraving of *Sneewittchen* (Snow White), made by one of the Grimm Bothers, Ludwig Emil, in 1825. In section nine of 'The True Story of Eleanor Marx in Ten Parts', the ashes of Eleanor Marx are placed inside a cupboard with glass doors, like a version of Snow White in her glass coffin.

The Giving Away of Emma Bovary By Several Hands · This is a list of six English versions of one line in Flaubert's *Madame Bovary*. The line is spoken by Emma's father, when he realises that Charles Bovary is about to ask for her hand in marriage. Strictly speaking the title of my poem is incorrect, because she is still Emma Rouault at this stage in the story. The translators are respectively: Lydia Davis, Alan Russell, Eleanor Marx, Geoffrey Wall, Adam Thorpe, Gerard Hopkins.

Who is He? · Based on information in Francis Steegmuller's biography of Flaubert, *Flaubert and Madame Bovary* (1947).

Are You Looking? · This poem uses phrases from *Madame Bovary*, trans. Geoffrey Wall (2003). Flaubert once wrote in a letter: 'I derive almost voluptuous sensations from the mere act of seeing' (1845), and it has been suggested that his descriptions of Emma are extremely voyeuristic. The first sentence in the novel to be spoken directly by Emma is '*Cherchez-vous quelque chose?*' ('Are you looking for something?'), though we have been closely observing her for some time before this. One of the earliest comments made about Emma in the book is by Charles's first wife, who says, '*Ce n'est pas la peine de faire tant de fla-fla*', translated by Wall as 'So much for all that la-di-da of hers'.

The Stenographer · This poem uses quotes from the Speech for the Prosecution and the Speech for the Defence in the 1857 trial of *Madame Bovary*, as recorded by Flaubert's stenographer (trans. Evelyn Gendel, 1964). The phrase '*elle meurt dans tout le prestige de sa jeunesse*' (she dies in all of the glamour of her youth') was part of the Speech for the Prosecution.

Faithful Henry · See 'The Frog King, Or Iron Henry' in *The Original Folk and Fairy Tales of the Brothers Grimm: The Complete First Edition*, trans. Jack Zipes (2014). At the end of the story about the frog who turns into a prince and marries the princess, there is a small section about the prince's 'Faithful Henry'.

Bachmann's Warbler · This poem combines information about the poet Ingeborg Bachmann and the small yellow-and-black bird called Bachman's Warbler.

Portrait of a Writer · See Gisèle Freund's 1939 photograph of Virginia Woolf. Freund said that her impression of Woolf was of a 'frail' and 'luminous' woman, 'the very incarnation of her prose'. In her diaries, Woolf wrote that posing for the camera was a 'violation of her purity'.

Drama Lessons for Young Girls · This poem conflates three experiences: a visit to an exhibition at the Ashmolean Museum, of classical sculpture *Gods in Colour*; listening to a news report on the failure of authorities in Oxfordshire to act on claims of sexual abuse of young girls; attending a lecture given by playwright Margaret Wilkinson on how to read a script.

Rehearsing Strindberg · This poem uses stage directions and lines from August Strindberg's *Miss Julie* trans. Michael Meyer (1964).

The Sad Tale of Hansel and Gretel · See 'Clever Hans' in *Brothers Grimm*, trans. Zipes. See also Margitt Lehbert's introduction to *The Poems of Georg Trakl* (2007).

'Oh my little Eleanor...' · This poem draws on answers written on a game sheet by ten-year old Eleanor Marx, during a family game of 'Confession'. See Holmes.

Karl Marx's Daughters Play on the Ouija Board · The characters in this poem are based on the Marx sisters Laura and Eleanor. The questions and answers are based on information about Eleanor's relationship with Edward Aveling.

The Tragic Death of Eleanor Marx · This poem uses phrases from several versions of the suicide scene in *Madame Bovary* (see also note to 'The True Story of Eleanor Marx in Ten Parts', above).

Acknowledgements

Thanks are due to the editors of the following publications, in which some of these poems have appeared: *Ambit, Blackbox Manifold, Currently & Emotion, Granta, The Honest Ulsterman, Locomotive, The Manchester Review, Modern Poetry in Translation, Poetry* (Chicago), *Poetry Ireland Review, Poetry Prescriptions, PN Review, Poetry Review, tender, The Times Literary Supplement.*

Thanks to the Arts Council Ireland for awarding me a Literary Arts Bursary to help research and write this collection.